Philosophy and Education

Max Black, William K. Frankena
Thomas F. Green, R. M. Hare, Paul H. Hirst
Michael Oakeshott, Ralph Barton Perry
R. S. Peters, Kingsley Price, Gilbert Ryle
Israel Scheffler, Harold Weisberg, Morton White

Boston

Allyn and Bacon, Inc.

Second Edition

Philosophy and Education

Modern Readings

Edited, with comments, by **Israel Scheffler**

Victor S. Thomas Professor of Education and Philosophy
Harvard University

Library of Congress catalog card number: 66-20642

Printed in the United States of America

Third printing . . . March, 1970

To my mother and father

Preface to the First Edition

The aim of this book is to present current philosophical methods in application to educational problems. It does not purport to provide another system of educational doctrine, nor to set forth another comparison of such systems. It is not intended to yield a practical program for the guidance of the schools. Rather, it focuses attention on underlying conceptual problems which confront those who would understand what education is, how it is best talked about, and what sorts of reasoning are appropriate in educational contexts. These problems it approaches with methods of analysis which have won wide acceptance in recent philosophy but which have not, so far, been sufficiently employed with reference to education. It is hoped that the book will thus contribute toward the establishment of closer relations between "general" philosophy and the philosophy of education: relations which would enrich the former by diversifying the scope of its methods and which would strengthen the latter by bringing its foundations under intensive new cultivation.

I wish to thank the authors and publishers for their cooperation. I am happy to acknowledge the encouragement and stimulation I have received from Dean Francis Keppel of the Harvard

Graduate School of Education, and I am grateful to Professor Robert Ulich and Dr. Morris L. Cogan for helpful advice. To the Harvard Foundation for Advanced Study and Research I am indebted for a grant for secretarial and research assistance. Mrs. Harriet Sachs Cronheim helped me in a preliminary exploration of the available literature and made a number of valuable suggestions.

I want, finally, to thank my wife for her frank and critical judgments of my writing, as well as for many discussions (which she has undoubtedly forgotten by now but which I have not) concerning the purposes and composition of this book.

Israel Scheffler

1958

Note to the Second Edition

For help in the preparation of the manuscript for the second edition, I wish to thank Mr. Peter F. Carbone, Jr., and Mrs. Dorothy Spotts.

I. S.

1966

Contents

Philosophy and Education

Introduction to the First Edition

THIS BOOK IS INTENDED both to illustrate and to stimulate the application of newer philosophical approaches to education. Such a purpose, natural though it is, flies in the face of both institutional and intellectual custom in calling for serious converse between professional philosopher and professional educator. For although such converse is fairly frequent between philosopher and scientist, between philosopher and man of letters, and between philosopher and theologian, the philosopher and educator typically face each other as relative strangers on the academic landscape who, when they do talk to each other, speak with the distant politeness of those who have urgent business elsewhere.

This distance, to be sure, is part of a larger pattern, and does not separate merely the professional philosopher from the educator in this country. For complex historical reasons,[1] those identified with the liberal arts, generally, have become estranged from those whose main concerns relate to our expanding educational system

[1] See "On the Conflict Between the 'Liberal Arts' and the 'Schools of Education'," by H. M. Jones, F. Keppel, and R. Ulich, *American Council of Learned Societies Newsletter*, Vol. 5, No. 2, pp. 17–38.

and the training of its teachers. In the case of philosophy, however, two facts render its current remoteness from education especially ironic. One is the fact that the very beginnings of philosophical reflection were rooted in educational concerns, and that the deepest problems of knowledge have since largely been taken also as problems of learning and thinking. The second is the fact that philosophy is currently undergoing rapid growth, both in the range and subtlety of its methods of analysis, and in the applicability of these methods to a variety of special fields. Together, these facts make it plain that the present academic rift between "pure" or "general" philosophy and the philosophy of education is an accident justified neither by historical precedent nor by practical reason.

The essays to follow will, it is hoped, contribute to the overcoming of this rift by showing how serious interest in educational concepts and issues may be fused with no less serious concern for philosophical clarity and rigor. The word "fused" is crucial here. For the academic rift in question has not completely obliterated all connection between "general" philosophy and philosophy of education. Rather, by reducing sympathetic two-way communication, it has rendered this connection mechanical, external, forced. Some proponents of "general" philosophical positions have, for example, not hesitated to derive so-called implications for education with little serious attention to educational phenomena in their own right. This has given educators the natural impression that they have nothing essential to contribute to the philosophical consideration of their field, that they can but humbly receive what the "general" philosophers freely offer and strive conscientiously to apply it in their daily work. Since, moreover, these philosophers are *independently* divided on the very doctrines from which they draw their educational imperatives, educators have been put the awkward task of having to decide, on grounds they are allegedly not professionally competent to judge, which of several conflicting sets of educational "implications" to adopt as their own guides to thought and action. Small wonder that they have been offered philosophy of education largely as an array of abstract "isms," neatly classified and examined for educational "implications," all displayed attractively side by side for the educators' unphilosophical choice. Small wonder, too, that from the educators' point of view, philosophy has thus often appeared arbitrary and artificial, peculiarly unreal when contrasted either with the actual work of the schools or with the concrete findings and directives of empirical research. Worst of all, the temptation to employ philosophy to intimidate educators by the brandishing of "big names" and doctrinal labels has tended to obscure the basic significance of philosophical *activity* as rational reflection, critical analysis of arguments and assumptions, systematic clarification of fundamental ideas.

It is to the furtherance of such activity with respect to education that this collection of essays is addressed, since it is the development of such activity which, in the editor's opinion, may best bring about the fusion spoken of earlier. Such fusion will indeed involve the connecting of philosophy with education, but since this is to be conceived not as one-way deduction of educational implications from general doctrines independently espoused but rather as the extension of philosophical methods of analysis to educational contexts, it will presuppose serious attention to these contexts and will aim at clarifying and deepening our awareness of their significance.

This is not, of course, to deny that the *results* of philosophical inquiry in other areas may be relevant to the deeper understanding of educational contexts. Rather, it is to insist that such relevance can be rightly appraised only when these contexts themselves have been subjected to independent philosophical scrutiny. Nor is it implied that a primary concern for the clarification of educational matters by philosophical methods absolves the philosopher of education from the need to strive for the broadest knowledge of philosophic thought, both past and present. What is implied is merely that such knowledge in itself is not sufficient—that it must be used not as a substitute for detailed analysis of educational contexts but rather as a source of clues as to how best to carry on this analysis, the success of the whole enterprise to be judged by the adequacy and fruitfulness of the latter.

Finally, the phrase "educational contexts" must not be wrongly construed as referring to primarily practical problems or difficulties agitating those who shape the policies of our schools. Such limitation would falsely suggest that it is conceptual confusion which is largely responsible for these problems, or falsely promise that philosophical clarification will be of direct practical use in solving them. But these problems typically involve much more (or much less) than conceptual difficulty and the influence of philosophy on educational practice must correspondingly be conceived as much more subtle and indirect.

To call for the application of philosophical methods to education is, therefore, not at all to hold forth a panacea for the practical difficulties attending the schooling of the young. Rather, such a proposal aims explicitly at improving our *understanding* of education by clarification of our conceptual apparatus—the ways in which we formulate our beliefs, arguments, assumptions, and judgments concerning such topics as learning and teaching, character and intellect, subject-matter and skill, desirable ends and appropriate means of schooling. Clarification of this sort is likely, of course, to affect our educational practice indirectly, but it cannot in itself substitute for concrete factual information about the context of such practice nor for firm moral commitment to goals that may direct it. In applying philosophical methods of analysis, we are, then, concerned *directly* with solving intellectual rather than practical difficulties—with removing the perplexities that arise in our attempt to say systematically and clearly what we are doing in education and why.

It has already been remarked that the *fusion* of philosophical and educational concerns, in the sense here discussed, represents a departure from the approach taken by those who "deduce" educational implications from general philosophical doctrines in unilateral fashion. It must now equally be stressed (especially in the light of what was said in the previous paragraph) that such fusion departs just as radically from the picture often projected, by educational practitioner and researcher alike, of the ideal role of the philosopher of education. This picture, possibly an educator's reaction to the abstract "deductive" approach often taken by "general" philosophers, gives the philosopher of education responsibility for enunciating basic values and formulating intermediate objectives for educational institutions.

Such an assignment, insofar as it acknowledges the important place of moral considerations in education, is of course admirable, as well as complimentary to the philosophers. But it is likely to embarrass many of them as well, betraying, for all its good intentions, an unreal estimate of the philosopher's capacities and limitations. The assignment of value-determination to the philosopher on the one hand absurdly exaggerates his moral wisdom and good judgment, whereas on the other it underestimates the contribution he *can* make by his professional striving for generality and system, clarity and logical rigor.

To take the first point first, value-determination cannot plausibly be considered the exclusive responsibility of any specialist, not even the specialist in generality. It cannot be professionalized and given over to experts, for there are no experts in moral sensitivity, wisdom, and ethical judgment. The research specialist in education is understandably anxious to limit his own technical competence to the determination of appropriate means, and hence naturally thinks of the complementary formulation of ends as the job of some other specialist, i.e., the philosopher. But the philosopher, though flattered, must in all modesty resist the role of expert moral guide while accepting his share of *every* man's obligation to take moral issues seriously and to judge wisely and well. He ought, even more, to try as philosopher to clarify the structure of moral decision, to contribute intellectual perspective to the consideration of urgent moral choices of the day, and to stimulate a sharper awareness of their implications. But to those who ask him, as alleged expert, to determine society's ends for them so that they can get on with the study of means, his answer must be a critical analysis of this very demand rather than an obligingly direct reply.

Such an analysis, indeed, exemplifies the positive contribution the philosopher of education *can* make when he conceives his function to be neither the spinning out of implications from general doctrines nor the authoritative pronouncement of basic and intermediate values for the guidance of schools. He can try to clarify our fundamental ways of thinking about education: the concepts we employ, the inferences we make, and the choices we express. He can render explicit the criteria of judgment we use in reaching educational decisions. He can test our common assumptions indirectly by striving for a systematic picture that will embrace them all. He can analyze the major positions taken on issues of educational policy by exposing their premises, consequences, and alternatives. In sum, he can improve our *understanding* of educational contexts and the problems they generate.

A detailed word must here be devoted to the approach that the philosopher of education is likely to bring to his task at the present time. It is no secret that a good part of recent philosophy has been critical, scientific, and analytic in temper,[2] and that, to a large extent, it has been written in a new key,[3] that of language and symbolism. It is far less well understood, however, that this new key represents not a radically different sphere of interest, not a turning away from older and grander issues, but rather, at most, a new way of looking at problems and, at the least, a new level of precision in traditional ways. There is no doubt, to be sure, that in the wake of recent philosophical developments certain older problems have been largely discarded as spurious and certain others have come to be regarded as now solved. Such elimination of problems, however, by no means implies a sharp break with philosophic tradition; it is rather a natural effect of acquiring a new perspective on it, and new tools for working within it. After all, unless we are to construe philosophy as inherently incapable of advance, our aim must be precisely to develop new points of view and better tools with which to attack its problems. That we have recently seen a reordering, a reformulation, and a resifting of such problems is thus a sign of the vitality, not of the abandonment, of the philosophic tradition.

Perhaps one of the main reasons why such an obvious point has been obscured lies in the difficulty of the notion of "language," a notion that figures centrally in recent developments. Languages are clearly as natural elements of our world as earthquakes, flowers, or revolutions. They can thus be taken, in themselves, as objects of scientific investigation, with a view toward determining their structures, origins, and relationships to other parts of the physical and human scene. Such scientific study of language seems, however, no more relevant to traditional problems of philosophy than other major branches of scientific scholarship. To say merely that recent philosophy has become preoccupied with linguistic matters is therefore likely to suggest that it has turned its back on such questions as the nature of truth and knowledge, existence and causality, the good and the right, and has instead taken up the scientific study of grammar and philology. In order to dispel this suggestion, one must also specify the sense in which linguistic considerations are thought to be philosophically important.

2 M. White, *The Age of Analysis*. New York: The New American Library of World Literature, Inc., 1955.

3 S. K. Langer, *Philosophy in a New Key*. Cambridge: Harvard University Press, 1942.

Though various factional formulations are current, we can perhaps briefly state the essential point to be the "transparency" of language: the fact that, unlike earthquakes, flowers, and revolutions, languages are our vehicles for describing the world, for expressing our beliefs and judgments, for pronouncing preferences and obligations, for systematizing our philosophical convictions and scientific information. To study our language with a view toward clarifying and improving its functioning as such a vehicle, as recent philosophy has done, is, in an important sense, to "look through" language at the whole range of traditional issues, issues concerning fundamental notions such as truth, belief, and judgment, value and obligation, intuition and verification. The linguistic philosopher, then, is not striving to develop a scientific theory *of* languages, but rather to clarify, improve, or systematize the languages in which we express our scientific theories concerning any of a variety of subjects, as well as our common-sense beliefs, our judgments, inferences, evaluations, and convictions. It is this purpose that keeps him clearly within the philosophic tradition.

The previous paragraph made reference to factional differences within the camp of linguistic philosophers. There are, in addition, further differences between philosophers who self-consciously invoke the notion of language-analysis in performing and in describing their work and philosophers who do not, although they are also appropriately described as analytical in approach. The analytical temper of recent philosophizing is not the hallmark of linguistic philosophies alone, but represents rather the converging emphases of a variety of trends, including, besides the explicitly linguistic movements, varieties of realism, pragmatism, and the philosophy of science. What these and still other recent approaches basically have in common is what might be described as an "inductive" way of going about things, a willingness to tackle single problems in piecemeal fashion, and a subjection of general assertions to the twin tests of fact and logical clarity. The specific methods employed differ, of course, but there is a unanimous distrust of large generalizations about the universe, of attempts to interpret all of human life in terms of a single idea, of systems whose air of profundity and deductive strength is bought at the expense of a disparagement of common experience. In addition, there is hostility not alone to philosophizing that in practice reveals impatience with evidence or that, in its haste to edify, substitutes rhetoric for reasons, but also, and above all, to philosophies that scorn reasoned discourse in principle, that glory in the vague and the subjective, and make a virtue of paradox.

It is a whole cluster of procedures and attitudes, then, that roughly defines the analytical temper mentioned earlier, a temper all the more significant in recent philosophy because it is *not* peculiar to any single faction, but unites a variety of philosophers in the concern for rigorous standards of clarity and cogency. Surely, for the development of educational philosophy, it is the emphasis on clarity, logic, and evidence that is of *fundamental* relevance, rather than the partisan claims of associated schools. Accordingly, though the label "analytic" is often reserved by philosophers for explicitly linguistic trends, it is here used to signal the general temper above described and the whole variety of methods employed by those it animates.

It would be exceedingly difficult, and in itself probably misleading, to present to the general reader a catalogue of these methods, purporting to describe each adequately and precisely. It is hoped that the essays to follow will themselves, and in a much more illuminating way, bring home the import of a variety of methods of philosophical analysis in application, moreover, to educational questions. Nevertheless, a brief general word about some of these methods may be welcome at this point, not in order to provide exhaustive definition, but merely to point to salient emphases.

One method of analysis, which we may call "structural," starts by noting as carefully as possible the logical structure of the position or argument under examination, filling in omitted steps and likely assumptions. This is then followed by a critical examination to determine not only whether the argument is formally consistent and sound, i.e., whether its conclusions indeed follow from its premises or are rendered likely by them, but also to what extent these premises themselves are supported by available evidence. Such a procedure is not merely useful for critical purposes; by calling attention to the structure of inadequate positions it is likely to suggest positive steps that need to be taken in order to reformulate them and bring them into line with relevant evidence.

Such a positive purpose underlies also what has been called the method of "rational reconstruction," which tries to render explicit the rules and special standards governing our valid inferences in given domains. Originally developed in connection with the scientists' procedures, this method is by no means limited to science. Wherever decisions are deliberate, and rational discussion possible, it is pertinent to investigate the factors entering into such decisions and the criteria by which they are judged, as well as the standards to which such rational discussion appeals. This method is as relevant to moral choice as it is to scientific judgment, and it seems especially well suited to educational contexts, where decisions on what and how to teach appear related in quite definite ways to a variety of considerations and where arguments over the justification of such decisions make appeal to certain specific criteria.

Aside from the methods we have just considered, which are concerned with the logical *structure* of particular arguments or types of inference, a number of methods concern rather the clarification of specific concepts. One such method, which we might denote as "contextual," stresses the dependence of concepts upon the practical contexts in which they are used. This method consists, then, in a careful examination of the functioning of given terms within specific situations, of the purposes their introduction serves within such situations, and of the criteria such situations specify for their correct application. This method is especially sensitive to confusions arising from careless use of the same term in more than one practical context, when appropriate contextual limitations are ignored. Since educational terms are often employed in scientific, moral, and institutional contexts in a variety of ways, the relevance of this "contextual" method of analysis here is obvious.

A number of methods, which we may term "semantic," focus on the typical uses of terms or concepts in ordinary language. These uses are studied not by direct reference to practical context, but rather as revealed by the semantic network of the language, i.e., by what it *makes sense* to say with given concepts and by what it does not. Such study, in elucidating the patterns of semantic connection in which important concepts are embedded, enables us to criticize those arguments whose persuasiveness and confusion both derive from violation of the appropriate patterns. Semantic methods, potently used to criticize classical philosophic doctrines, have hardly been applied at all to educational notions and are likely to have illuminating results in this area.

Finally, mention must be made of "explicative" methods, whose object is not primarily to describe standard uses of current concepts, but rather to refine and explain these concepts systematically so as to render them unambiguous, precise, and theoretically adequate. The refined products of explicative methods must be similar in certain basic respects to their natural originals; they must be, recognizably, precision-made idealizations of these originals. Yet for the sake of superiority in expressive or theoretical power, "explication" feels free to deviate considerably from the actual uses of concepts in ordinary language. Its systematic emphasis, furthermore, forces upon us considerations of consistency, as well as the adequacy of the basic concepts used to explain all the rest, and it brings to light alternative routes of explanation and expression.

It should go without saying that as here briefly described, the foregoing methods are "ideal types," not to be expected in their pure forms in concrete philosophic discourses. Nor can they, once learned, be applied mechanically to particular problems; their use requires judgment and tact, intelligence and wisdom. Their schematic descriptions are offered here as aids in the learning of philosophy, not as self-sufficient philosophic tools.

So much by way of a brief word about methods of analysis as preliminary orientation to the selections themselves. These selections do not, as a whole, represent what is typically taken as philosophy of education currently, nor were they uniformly conceived by their authors originally as efforts in the philosophy of education. This indicates, however, much less about the writings themselves than about current conceptions of educational philosophy. If a fusion of philosophical method and approach with educational concerns is to come about, it will, in any event, need to break through the boundaries of these conceptions, and stimulate new ways of looking at philosophy and philosophers of education. Accordingly, the selection of the writings to follow was wholly indifferent to the official label borne by each, as to field. The guiding criteria were rather the following: (a) concern with some important aspect of education, or area intimately related to education; (b) clarity and challenge of presentation; (c) exemplification of some significant philosophic approach or method with wider bearings. Exhaustiveness can hardly be claimed either for the choice of topics or methods (if the notion of exhaustiveness indeed makes sense in this context), but it *was* hoped that a significant variety of both subjects and methods of analysis would be represented. It was also hoped that some sense of the continuity and lively growth of philosophical analysis might be conveyed by the inclusion of selections from the work of younger as well as older writers. Teachers will be interested to know that practically all these selections have been used in courses in the philosophy of education at Harvard. It hardly needs saying, however, that there is nothing pedagogically sacred about the order in which the selections appear here, especially in view of the wide range of topics, methods, and levels of difficulty represented.

It must, finally, be emphasized that the essays do *not* represent a new school of substantive educational doctrine; the reader who searches them for an overarching and consistent system will be hopelessly misled. They exemplify, rather, philosophic methods of analysis in action. The student who profits from their example in constructing his own system of beliefs may be better equipped than he was at the outset, but he will find himself in the middle, not at the end, of his intellectual journey.

Many anthologies represent harvests, fulfillments, symbols of lines of investigation that have proven fruitful over the years. The present anthology is not one of these. It is rather in the nature of a promise or, if you like, a hypothesis about the kind of investigation philosophy of education might become. If it stimulates others to test the promise, to try the hypothesis in fact, it will have served its purpose despite its many shortcomings.

Israel Scheffler

1958

Introduction to the Second Edition

In the eight years that have passed since the appearance of the first edition, there have been considerable changes in the situation to which it was addressed. The rift between professional education and the arts and sciences has perceptibly narrowed, and academic scholars and researchers have, to an increasing degree, begun to take seriously the stubborn problems of educational development in the contemporary world. There is still much to be done in this direction, to be sure, but the indications of progress already achieved, in the surmounting of old barriers and the elimination of isolating preconceptions, are undeniable.

Regarding more particularly philosophical concerns, noticeable progress has been made in overcoming the hampering division between general philosophy and the philosophy of education, the former showing an increased awareness of educational issues and the latter a growing appreciation of the reach of general philosophical developments. All in all, the application of newer philosophical approaches to educational topics has become more widespread, and there has been increasing recognition of the importance of bringing together the concerns of the contemporary philosophical analyst with those of the thoughtful educator interested in clarifying the concepts guiding his practice.

Here, too, much remains to be done in the same direction. Yet, unlike the situation only eight short years ago, there is now a recognizable and growing corpus of writings dealing relatively directly with educational matters in the spirit of general developments in philosophy. The quality of such work has been uneven, to be sure. There have been wooden, as well as insightful, applications of analytic methods, and pointless, as well as significant, methodological exercises. Unevenness may, however, be expected in any new intellectual enterprise of comparable scope. The important fact, it seems to me, is that the enterprise has clearly begun and is being carried forward, that the old walls are crumbling, and that a freer and friendlier communication between education and philosophy is being developed.

The need is no longer urgent, as it was in 1958, simply to demonstrate the possibility that "serious interest in intellectual concepts and issues may be fused with no less serious concern for philosophical clarity and rigor." That lesson has been learned. The current task is to move from possibilities and programs to substantive issues. What is primarily needed, in my opinion, is fresh constructive work on the many concrete problems of educational thought that await philosophical treatment.

The foregoing reflections serve at least partially to explain the changes in the present edition. First of all, this edition contains some newer materials that represent recent tendencies, as well as some basic selections of the original edition, retained for the sake of continuity and intrinsic interest. Secondly, there is a more direct focus on the substance of education in the present edition. The 1958 version, in order to picture the unrealized promise of a fusion between philosophical analysis and educational concerns, included some selections dealing not directly with education but rather with closely related areas of importance. In the present edition, these selections have been largely supplanted by others with a more direct educational bearing. Finally, whereas the first edition touched on a wide variety of educational topics in an effort to open doors to the broadest development of the field, the present edition presents a more selective development of educational topics, in the confidence that the main doors are now, in any event, open. Such a course has, unfortunately, necessitated the omission of further selections from the first edition. However, whatever loss in scope is thereby sustained is, I believe, more than offset by a gain in integration. (The theme of moral education, for example, now provides a unifying thread running through the book.)

The plan of the sections is as follows: The first two sections provide a general introduction to education and the study of education. The third section offers discussions of the central notion of teaching and its varieties, introducing reference to both cognitive and moral dimensions. The fourth section is concerned primarily with notions of cognition and competence, and their relations to performance. (Drawn from one of the most influential books in recent philosophy, the selections in this fourth section have stimulated a large body of comment and have, in one way or another, affected the thinking of a great many contemporary philosophers. It seemed to me more desirable, however, to reprint the original selections than to replace them with any of the critical discussions contingent upon them.) The fifth section offers fundamental and interrelated considerations of moral education, considerations that are foreshadowed in the third section and elsewhere and are further ramified in the sixth section on political and religious education.

I remarked in the Introduction to the First Edition that its selections did not, as a whole, reflect typical conceptions of philosophy of education, "nor were they uniformly conceived by their authors originally as efforts in the philosophy of education." That observation applies also to the present edition; however, many more of the selections in the present, as compared with the earlier, edition have in fact been written as explicit contributions to the philosophy of education, and current construals of the field are changing in ways that are hospitable to its guiding conception. The idea of a "fusion of philosophical method and approach with educational concerns" has, at any rate, gained an initial foothold. If it is not to falter, it must now be strengthened by constructive work on issues of theoretical and practical significance.

Israel Scheffler

1966

I

Concepts of Education

Editor's Comments

As with all major branches of human culture, educational activity is articulated, organized, and executed with the aid of distinctive clusters of concepts functioning in a variety of ways. Some of these concepts are relatively specialized or technical, pertaining primarily to limited phases of practice. Others are more general, figuring widely in description of fundamental processes, institutions, or ideologies, in formulation of basic goals and programs, in inference and argumentation underlying important decisions. It is these general concepts, so intimately related to the quality and direction of educational activity, that attract the philosopher's attention. He wants to make sense of them, or rather, to see if and how they make sense when subjected to systematic and impartial scrutiny conducted far from the heat of action. Such an examination may facilitate the discovery of weak assumptions and controlling analogies usually suppressed in practice, it may expose normally unnoticed confusions, it may suggest fruitful comparisons and improved ways of thinking about education.

The two essays to follow represent quite different (though not incompatible) emphases in the philosophic clarification of general educational concepts. Professor Perry's selection is taken from a book in which he systematically discusses not education alone, but all major phases of organized social life. He is thus mainly concerned with describing the essential features of education as an element of culture. In so doing, he presents a concise overall view, explaining in order some fundamental concepts and distinctions widely current in thinking about education—for example, the notions of cultural transmission, of formal versus informal education, of a science of education, of moral education, of education for democracy, and of liberal education. Attention should be called especially to his treatment of the notion of indoctrination and of the widespread argument that no well-defined educational scheme can avoid authoritarian imposition of values upon the young.

Professor Black's essay is an attempt to shed light on educational processes by drawing an extended analogy with artistic creation. He suggests that educational theories are often channeled in specific directions by root metaphors that derive their plausibility from valid but inevitably limited parallels with other fields. Nor is this, in his opinion, a mistake, since such metaphors help to effect a preliminary organization of reflection. The remedy for limited comparisons is not the avoidance of analogy altogether (if this is indeed possible) but rather the deliberate construction of diverse analogies which, not paradoxically, may illumine the unique character of a subject precisely by exhibiting its multiple similarities to a host of others. Thus, to take an independent example, many philosophers have treated ethics as analogous to science. Others have compared it to the law. Still others have exhibited its similarities to aesthetic criticism and some have insisted on the dynamic force that ethical statements share with commands. To see in what ways ethics is analogous to all these areas, it has been argued, is precisely to avoid reducing it to any, and to gain a fuller appreciation of its individual character. Some philosophers have indeed suggested such deliberate "analogizing" as a primary tool of philosophy. Be that as it may, Black's exploration of "education as art and discipline" may serve as a model of perceptive comparison, as well as a reminder of the significance of metaphor in educational theory.

1. Education and the
Science of Education[*]

Ralph Barton Perry
Harvard University

IN THE FUNDAMENTAL SENSE, education is the cultural process by which successive generations of men take their places in history. Nature has assigned an indispensable role to education through the prolongation of human infancy, and through the plasticity of human faculties. By nature man is not equipped for life but with capacities that enable him to learn how to live. Since it is generally agreed that acquired characteristics are not inherited education assumes the full burden of bringing men "up to date," creating "the modern man" of the 1953, or any other latest, model. Through education men acquire the civilization of the past, and are enabled both to take part in the civilization of the present, and make the civilization of the future. In short, the purpose of education is three-fold: inheritance, participation, and contribution.

It is quite conceivable that any one of these elements should be so accentuated as to exclude or obscure the other two: as when education is conceived as a mere deposit and preservation of the

* This selection appeared originally in Ralph Barton Perry, *Realms of Value*. Cambridge, Massachusetts: Harvard University Press, 1954, pp. 411–414, 421–424, 425–436. Reprinted by permission.